Prayer Patterns

LIN JOHNSON

VICTOR BOOKS

A DIVISION OF SCRIPTURE PRESS PUBLICATIONS INC.
USA CANADA ENGLAND

Editor: Carolyn Nystrom
Cover Design: Grace K. Chan Mallette
Cover Photo: William Koechling

Recommended Dewey Decimal Classification: 248:4
Suggested Subject Heading: PERSONAL RELIGION: PRAYER

Library of Congress Catalog Card Number: 93-19786
ISBN: 1-56467-193-2

1 2 3 4 5 6 7 8 9 10 Printing/Year 97 96 95 94 93

CONTENTS

THE TAPESTRY COLLECTION

Michelle Booth
Gold in the Ashes
Eight Studies on Wisdom from Job

Marion Duckworth
Renewed on the Run
Nine Studies on 1 Peter

Lin Johnson
Prayer Patterns
Ten Prayers to Weave the Fabric of Your Life

Vicki Lake
Restored in the Ruins
Eight Studies on Nehemiah

Ellen E. Larson and David V. Esterline
More than a Story
Nine Studies on the Parables of Jesus

RuthAnn Ridley
Every Marriage is Different
Eight Studies on Key Biblical Marriages

Beth Donigan Seversen
Mirror Image
Eight Studies from Colossians

INTRODUCTION

Browse in any Christian bookstore or church library, and you will notice an abundance of books on prayer.
There are books about:
—why we should pray
—methods of prayer
—how prayer changes us and the world
—how to listen to God
—what the Bible teaches about prayer
—hindrances to prayer and what to do about them
—scheduling prayer times
—group prayer
—individual prayer
You will even find prayer notebooks or journals in which to record your own prayers.

This book is different. It focuses on written prayers in the Bible and what we can learn from their structures and content in relationship to 20th century situations.

As you complete these studies, you may be surprised at what you learn about prayer. I was! I trust that this book will guide you into prayer-changing insights.

Some of these prayers, like Matthew 6:9-13, are old friends. You can quote them in your sleep. Others you may have glossed over in your Bible reading hardly noticing that they are prayers. But don't let familiarity rob you of learning. Try to read each biblical prayer as though for the first time. Even though the study questions direct your attention to the structure and elements of the prayers, don't miss the rich truths they teach about God and our relationship with Him.

Before you begin, ask God to use these studies to enrich and expand your prayer life. May the biblical patterns become yours for a lifetime of talking with God.

Using This Study Guide

This guide is designed for individual use as well as for group study. So, whether you are using this book for personal study or as the basis for a group study, follow the instructions below regarding the purpose and use of each section in this guide.

Plan to study one prayer a week in order to allow yourself time to practice what you learn. Before beginning each study, pray that the Holy Spirit will help you understand what each Bible prayer teaches and how to follow its pattern as you pray for others and yourself.

Each chapter is divided into three sections:

❦ *Examining the Pattern* is a series of inductive Bible study questions designed to help you interact with the Bible text. You may want to complete each study in two or three sittings, rather than answer all the questions at once. Read each Bible passage carefully. Although the questions are based on the *New International Version*, you may find it helpful to read the prayers in one or two other translations as well. Then, instead of copying the Bible text, put the answers to the questions in your own words. Depend on the Holy Spirit to guide and help you with the application questions.

❦ *Fitting the Pattern* is a narrative section with commentary on the prayer you studied along with illustrations and applications.

❦ *Using the Pattern* contains guidelines for practicing the prayer pattern you studied and suggestions for daily prayer starters.

❦ A *Group Study Guide* at the end of this book provides a discussion outline for using his study guide in a group setting.

For Further Study

This book includes only twelve prayers from the Bible. There are dozens more to use as patterns for enriching your prayer life. So when you finish these studies, you may want to examine more. Check out the Book of Psalms, as well as Hannah's prayer in 1 Samuel 2:1-10; Solomon's in 1 Kings 8:22-53; Nehemiah's in Nehemiah 1; the Levites' in Nehemiah 9; Daniel's in Daniel 9:4-19; and Christ's in John 17.

1

WHEN YOU WANT TO IMPROVE YOUR PRAYER LIFE

Matthew 6:5-13

EXAMINING THE PATTERN

1. If someone listened to your prayers for a week, how would that person describe your prayer life? Mark each of the line graphs to show where your prayers fall between the two extremes.

   Focus:

   Own needs   Others' needs
   |___|___|___|___|___|___|___|___|___|___|___|

   Kinds of prayer: thanksgiving, worship, requests, confession, other

   One   Many
   |___|___|___|___|___|___|___|___|___|___|___|

To find out how to balance your prayer life, complete this study on Christ's model prayer.
Read Matthew 6:5-8.

2. Why did Jesus give this prayer pattern to His disciples?

Read Matthew 6:9-13.

3. With what element of prayer does this model begin? (v. 9) Why do you think that Jesus began that way?

4. How is God's name "hallowed" or made holy?

5. What is the second element of Christ's prayer? (v. 10)

6. Why is submission to God's will important?

How is it related to prayer requests?

7. What element of prayer does verse 11 represent?

8. Why do you think Jesus focused on food?

9. What element of prayer is included in verse 12?

Why is this element important to prayer?

10. In verse 13, what kind of request is stated?

Why is it important?

11. Although it is not included in the *New International Version*, many other translations end verse 13 with these words: "For Thine is the kingdom, and the power, and the glory, forever. Amen" (NASB). What element of prayer does this sentence represent?

How is this closing sentence related to the beginning of this prayer?

Why is this a fitting end to this model prayer?

12. What have you learned about the basic elements of prayer from Christ's model?

13. Why do you think Jesus put the prayer elements in this order?

14. How do your own prayers compare with this one?

15. What elements have you neglected recently in your prayers? Why?

16. Now that you've studied Christ's pattern, identify a change you want to make in the way you pray. Write it on page 71, *Changing the Pattern of My Prayers.*

FITTING THE PATTERN

It's easy to let our prayers get unbalanced. What we talk to God about tends to reflect our immediate concerns; we forget other elements of prayer. God wants us to take our concerns to Him. But He also desires our worship, praise, and submission. So Jesus taught this in His model prayer.

It's also easy to pray in generalities, such as "Bless my friend Jan today." Or "Forgive me if I sinned today." But Christ's model teaches us to pray more specifically. In His prayer, He gave guidelines.

Notice that Jesus began by addressing God as "Father in Heaven." He did not pray to some nebulous man upstairs but to His loving Father. Praying to our Father announces our relationship with Him, that we are His children because of faith in Jesus. (See John 1:12-13.) Our Father is the one true God who lives in heaven. When we pray, we need to focus first on God who is sovereign and has supernatural resources available for our use.

Furthermore, God is holy and deserves our worship. To make His name holy involves respecting Him for who He is, regarding Him as different from men—sinless, everywhere present, uncommon. It also includes honoring and revering Him, obeying Him, keeping His reputation untarnished by the way we live.

Instead of crashing breathlessly into God's presence with our wish list, Jesus taught us to begin prayer with worship. (There are, however, times when we need to abruptly call out to God for help.) But we must submit to God's sovereignty: "Your kingdom come, your will be done on earth as it is in heaven." We let God rule our lives, putting His will before our own. The more we study Scripture, the more we know of His will so that we can submit to Him.

In the next sentence, Jesus turned the focus of prayer from God to the one who prays. "Give us today our daily bread" is a general guideline for requesting that God meet our needs. It may be something as basic as food or as complex as solving a relationship conflict. Whatever we need, we should ask God for it. "Do not be anxious about anything, but in everything, by prayer and petition, with thanksgiving, present your requests to God," Paul wrote in Philippians 4:6. Praying about needs acknowledges that everything comes from God and that we are dependent on Him.

Not only should we request what we need, but we should also ask God for forgiveness for sin. John expressed this guideline like this: "If we confess our sins, he is faithful and just and will forgive us our sins and purify us from all unrighteousness" (1 John 1:9). In turn, we need to forgive others, "forgiving each other, just as in Christ God forgave you" (Ephesians 4:32). The final request Jesus mentioned is for guidance, particularly for victory over temptation.

After that, Christ concluded with more praise of God, going full circle from worship, to needs, and back to worship. Instead of requests being the predominant type of prayer, Christ sandwiched expression of need between praises of the God who is able to meet those needs. It's a pattern that reminds us of who we're talking to and why.

How balanced are your prayers? Have you slipped into one or two kinds of prayer while forgetting or ignoring others? If so, bring in the other elements of prayer that Jesus used in His own pattern.

USING THE PATTERN

Follow Christ's model as you pray today. Record your prayer below.
❧ Worship God.

❦ Submit to His will.

❦ Ask your requests.

❦ Confess your sins.

❦ Ask for guidance.

❦ Praise/worship God.

During the week, continue to follow Christ's model of prayer. Let yourself become comfortable with these varying forms of prayer. Summarize or write out your prayers below.

Day 1   Practice worshiping God. Tell Him of His great worth to you. Talk to Him about specific ways that you can make His name holy today.

Day 2   Talk to God about how you can submit to His will today.

Day 3   Ask God to show you any sins you need to confess; then do so. Also ask for grace to quickly forgive others who wrong you.

Day 4   Ask for God's guidance in specific areas, especially where you face temptation.

Day 5   Combine all the elements in Christ's model prayer as you pray today.

WHEN YOU'VE SINNED

Psalm 51

EXAMINING THE PATTERN

1. What's your first response when you sin? Why?

Compare your response to David's as you read about a time when he sinned and his subsequent prayer.

Read 2 Samuel 11:1–12:14 for the occasion that motivated the prayer in Psalm 51.
2. Briefly summarize the story.

Now read Psalm 51:1-6.
3. How did David begin this prayer?

4. Define God's mercy and compassion.

Why did David appeal to these characteristics of God?

5. What was David's attitude toward his sin?

6. Against whom had he sinned?

Why do you think David said that?

7. What did David know about God that made confession of his sin easier?

Read verses 7-12.
  8. After David confessed his sin, what did he ask God to do? List his requests in your own words.

Note: Hyssop is a plant with stiff branches that was used for dipping into blood to sprinkle it for cleansing. The Hebrews used hyssop at the first Passover (Exodus 12:21-23) and on healed lepers (Leviticus 14:2-7).

The Holy Spirit permanently indwells believers today so David's request in verse 11 is not relevant to us.

Read verses 13-17.
  9. What would David be able to do as a result of confessing his sin? Be specific.

10. Why couldn't he do these before confessing?

Read verses 18-19.

11. With what request did David end his prayer?

12. How is this request related to the rest of his prayer?

13. Identify several actions we take to try to atone for our sins today.

14. Why aren't these actions effective?

15. Why is confession to God the only way to receive real forgiveness for sin?

16. Now that you've studied David's pattern, identify a change you want to make in the way you pray. Write it on page 71, *Changing the Pattern of My Prayers.*

FITTING THE PATTERN

People react to sin in various ways. Kim, for example, denies her habit of lying. Barb and her husband rationalize cheating on their income tax forms. They tell themselves that the government takes too much money anyway. Kathy admits that her affair with a married man is sin, but she doesn't care. Janet excuses shoplifting at the grocery store as her means of economic survival. Sandy is immediately miserable after one of her verbal blasts. Chris says gossip and criticism are not so bad.

Three thousand years ago, David tried to hide his sin with Bathsheba by manipulating circumstances. When that did not work, he committed more sins. But months later, when Nathan the prophet pointed out his sins, David finally confessed.

God put David's confession in the Bible, at least in part, to teach us how to respond to sin. But David's prayer was made public before it became Scripture. According to the title, it was used in public worship. (How would you like your congregation to sing *your* confessions?)

When David confessed his sin, he did not approach God with a rehearsal of who he was (God's anointed king of His chosen people) or what he had done for God (lots). He did not try to rationalize or excuse his actions. He did not express a blase' attitude toward his sin. Instead, he asked for God's mercy and forgiveness.

David took his sin to God because he knew what God is like. He appealed to God on the basis of His loving and compassionate nature. God's love and forgiveness are greater than any sin we can commit, even adultery and murder.

Furthermore, David took responsibility for his sin: "For I know my transgressions, and my sin is always before me" (v. 3). He did not try to blame his sinful actions on someone else or on society. He did not say, "I couldn't help it. It wasn't my fault."

In addition, David recognized that his sin was against God: "Against you, you only, have I sinned and done what is evil in your sight" (v. 4). Although we usually don't think about it, all sin is foremost against God. God sets the standards. So even though our sin hurts us and others, God is the primary object of our offense. God is holy, without sin, and expects His children to be the same. Christ's disciple Peter wrote, "But just as he who called you is holy, so be holy in all you do; for it is written: 'Be holy, because I am holy' " (1 Peter 1:15-16).

After confessing his sin and asking for forgiveness, David focused on serving God. Because David had experienced God's love and forgiveness firsthand, he wanted to tell others about God so that they too could receive God's love. Besides, David determined to worship God's way—with a humble spirit and penitent heart.

Finally, conscious that his sin would affect generations to come, David prayed for his people. He wanted the people to know God's prosperity and protection in spite of what he had done. So David, the king, bowed to his own King—and brought his people with him.

How often do you think about the character of God when you confess your sin? And when was the last time you identified specific ways to serve God as soon as you had asked for cleansing and restoration? If your idea of confession has been narrow, try David's pattern. Your prayer life may never be the same.

USING THE PATTERN

Is there unconfessed sin in your life today? If so, write a prayer patterned after David's and pray it to God.

❧ Ask for forgiveness, appealing to God's character.

❧ Confess your guilt, acknowledging that you've sinned against God.

❧ Ask for cleansing and restoration of your relationship with God.

❧ Tell God what you will do as a result of being forgiven.

❧ Ask for other requests.

Continue to take care of sin the same way David did. Summarize or write out your prayers below.

Day 1   Ask God to bring any unconfessed sin to mind. Then deal with it in a biblical way.

Day 2   Reflect on God's loving and forgiving nature. Praise Him for being that way.

Day 3   Think about God's holiness. Thank Him that Christ's death bridged the huge gulf between Him and you as a sinner.

Day 4   Pray verse 10, "Create in me a pure heart, O God, and renew a steadfast spirit within me." Ask God to show you anything that prevents this prayer from being answered.

Day 5   Pray for opportunities to tell others about God's love and forgiveness.

WHEN YOU'RE GOING THROUGH TROUBLE

Psalm 138

Examining the Pattern

1. When you face a trial or problem, for what do you pray?

As you study Psalm 138, compare your prayers in times of trouble with David's.
Read verses 1-3.
2. How did David praise God?

3. For what reasons did he praise Him?

4. Describe God's love and faithfulness.

How do these character qualities help us praise Him?

5. What does it mean to be made "bold and stouthearted"?

Read verses 4-6.

6. Why will earthly rulers praise God?

7. What is the "glory of the Lord"?

How can our praise reflect God's glory?

8. Why is it comforting to know that the exalted God sees the lowly and proud?

Why would this fact evoke praise?

Read verses 7-8.

9. When David went through trials, of what was he confident? Why?

10. How does God preserve us in the midst of trouble?

11. Compare verse 8 with Philippians 1:6. How can the truth of these verses help us when we are going through a period of trouble?

12. What is the only request in this prayer?

How does it relate to experiencing trials?

13. On what did David focus when he was going through trials?

14. On what do you usually focus?

15. How can David's focus help you when you face trouble?

16. Now that you've studied David's pattern, identify a change you need to make in the way you pray. Write it on page 71, *Changing the Pattern of My Prayers.*

FITTING THE PATTERN

How do you normally react to trials? Check all that apply.

- ☐ Complain about the problems.
- ☐ Ask God why.
- ☐ Feel sorry for myself.
- ☐ Ask God for help.
- ☐ Look for ways to get out of them.
- ☐ Blame God.
- ☐ Blame someone else.
- ☐ Try to ignore them, hoping they will go away.
- ☐ Pray for a quick deliverance.
- ☐ Develop an anxiety attack.
- ☐ Thank God.
- ☐ Turn away from the Lord for awhile.
- ☐ Other: _____

As Psalm 138 attests, David had a different reaction from our normal response to pain. David had learned that praising God changes our focus from the problem to the One who has the power to deal with the situation and bring us through it.

Praise is potent. It brings us face to face with the God of the universe, the God who is in control of all situations. "As we express and strengthen our faith through praise, we enthrone God in our situation. We tune ourselves in to enjoy His sovereign sufficiency. God in turn manifests His presence on our behalf, in both inner and outer ways. He uses our trials as a stage on which He displays His love and power and faithfulness. As a result, His reality becomes evident both to us and to others who observe our lives" (Warren and Ruth Myers, *Praise: A Door to God's Presence*, Colorado Springs, CO: NavPress, 1987, pp. 33-34).

Praise in the midst of trials lifts us beyond the anxiety of the moment. Instead of anxiety, praise brings our focus to God who is at work even in the problems. "Praising God brings our hearts in line with His intentions, so that He can work in us more freely. It opens us to His will, so that we can cooperate with Him in His plan" (Myers, p. 129).

Several years ago, I experienced a devastating time of trouble that lasted for two years. Even today, those events still affect many areas of my life. One of the fallouts from that situation was losing my teaching job at a time when I had no savings. I was forced to live by faith, not knowing if checks from freelancing would arrive before bills were past due. My natural reaction was to feel sorry for myself and to question God.

But during that time, I read through the Book of Psalms. I also read two books about praising God, including the one quoted above. I began to deliberately practice praising God daily. As I focused my thoughts on who God is and what He is like, instead of on my problems, coping with the realities of my life at that time became much easier.

Praising God did not change the situation. It did not make the trouble go away. But it changed me. My attitude changed. My trust in God deepened. I got to know God better. And I discovered that praise can be addictive. Addictive in a good sense.

By the time David wrote Psalm 138, he already knew the value of praise during times of trouble. The predominant focus of this prayer is praise. In fact, it is not until the end of the psalm that we discover that the context for his praise was some kind of hardship. And even that reference points to God and His ability to give strength, to complete the work of redemption and grace He had already started in David's life.

USING THE PATTERN

What trial or problem are you currently facing?

In light of that trial, record a prayer patterned after David's:

❦ Thank God for who He is.

❦ Remember what He has done for you in past trials.

❦ Express your confidence in God's ability to help you through the trial.

❦ Ask God to keep working on your behalf.

During the week, continue to pray as David did, using the following guidelines. Summarize or write out your prayers below.

Day 1   Think about who God is. Praise Him for His character.

Day 2   Think about what God is like. Praise Him for these attributes, or characteristics.

Day 3   Reflect on what God has done for you in past times of trouble and thank Him.

Day 4   Ask God to give you greater confidence in Him when you face the troubles of your current week.

Day 5   Thank God that He is greater than your current hardships and that He has the power to meet your needs in spite of your circumstances.

WHEN THINGS ARE GOING WELL

1 Chronicles 29:1-19

EXAMINING THE PATTERN

1. How do you normally respond when things are going well? Why?

Look at how David reacted when life was good for him.
Read 1 Chronicles 29:1-9.
  2. What situation prompted David's prayer?

Read verses 10-13.
  3. What impresses you about the way David began his prayer of response to the people's actions?

  4. Why do you think he started this way?

  5. For what did he specifically praise God?

6. How does this description of God correspond to the situation?

Read verses 14-17.
7. After praising God, what did David next focus on?

8. How did he describe himself and the Jewish people?

9. How do these descriptions fit the situation that prompted his prayer?

10. Why did David mention his motives for giving?

Read verses 18-19.
11. What requests did David make of God? Why?

12. What progression of topics do you notice in this prayer?

13. Why do you think David put them in this order?

14. How might using this prayer pattern make a difference in your life?

15. Now that you've studied David's pattern, identify a change you need to make in your own way of praying. Write it on page 71, *Changing the Pattern of My Prayers.*

FITTING THE PATTERN

Generally, we're more aware of our need for God when we face difficulties than we are when times are good. Unless we try to shut God out with blame or anger, we instinctively cry out to Him in hard times. But when there are no conflicts, when life is good, it's easy to take God for granted. At such times, prayer often becomes less intense, more like duty. But it shouldn't. David demonstrated this publicly when he gave his son Solomon the plans and resources for the temple.

That day must have been a spiritual high for David. One of David's greatest desires was to build a permanent place to worship God, a place that reflected God's greatness. But because David was a man of war, God would not allow him to build that temple. Even so, David created elaborate plans for God's new house. He collected and donated materials so that Solomon, his son, could begin the building program as soon as he became king. Other national leaders also gave willingly and wholeheartedly of their resources. Yes, life was good that day. So David praised the Lord with great fervor. It was natural for him to do so in all kinds of situations—including times when things were going well.

It's evident from David's prayer that he knew God well. He mentioned a variety of attributes, or characteristics of God. In fact, we get the impression that words are too limiting to express the overflowing praise in David's heart.

Then David moved from God to himself. Once we grasp God's nature, we gain a more accurate perception of ourselves. Since the occasion of this prayer was giving for the Temple, David called attention to the source of all the good from which he and the leaders gave: God. All that we have is a gift from Him. What we do with it, as well as the motive behind our actions, is our gift to God.

Moving beyond praise and self-assessment, David closed his prayer with requests related to the occasion. Appropriately, they centered on right motives and right relationship with the God he had praised so profusely.

So even when things were going well, David recognized his need for God. It was not a time to develop independence. Rather, it was an opportunity to reflect on God's greatness and goodness and to reassess who he was in relationship to that God. Can you say the same?

USING THE PATTERN

Think about the good things God has been doing for you. Then write a prayer patterned after David's.

❧ Praise God for who He is and what He does. Be specific.

❧ Acknowledge who you are and your relationship with God.

❧ Ask God for any requests related to what He has been doing for you.

Continue using David's prayer pattern throughout the week. Summarize or write out your prayers below.

Day 1   Praise God for specific characteristics and actions. Use the first half of the alphabet (A–M) to add variety to your praise. For example, A—God, You are almighty; You can do anything. B—You build me up when I need encouragement.

Day 2   Continue to praise God, using the second half of the alphabet (N–Z).

Day 3   Reflect on who you are in God's eyes. Then tell Him your insights.

Day 4   Talk with God about your relationship with Him.

Day 5   In light of what God has done for you this week, tell Him your requests.

WHEN YOU'RE AFRAID

2 Chronicles 20:1-22

EXAMINING THE PATTERN

1. What causes you to be afraid?

2. When you're afraid, how and for what do you usually pray?

**Compare your prayers to Jehoshaphat's when he was afraid.
Read 2 Chronicles 20:1-5.**
　3. What situation prompted Jehoshaphat's prayer?

Read his prayer in verses 6-12.
　4. How did Jehoshaphat address God? (v. 6)

5. What do each of these descriptions tell us about God?

6. What did Jehoshaphat focus on after praising God? (v. 7)

7. Why did he remember this particular event? (v. 8)

8. On what basis did Jehoshaphat go to God? (vv. 8-9)

9. Next Jehoshaphat stated the problem (vv. 10-12). Why was he afraid?

10. What did Jehoshaphat ask God to do? Why?

11. What was Jehoshaphat's attitude as he made this request?

In this case, we find out God's response to Jehoshaphat's prayer. Read verses 13-22.
12. What did God tell Jehoshaphat and the people? (vv. 13-17)

13. How would God's response help them deal with their fear?

14. How did Jehoshaphat and the people respond to God's words? (vv. 18-21)

15. What did God do about the situation that alleviated Jehoshaphat's fear? (v. 22)

When did He begin to work?

16. Would you have prayed like Jehoshaphat in this situation? Why or why not?

17. Now that you've studied Jehoshaphat's pattern, identify a change you need to make in the way you pray. Write it on page 71, *Changing the Pattern of My Prayers*.

FITTING THE PATTERN

With every step forward, my fear increased. It was too late to back out; there were too many people in line behind me. *Why did I let Bill talk me into this?* I questioned. When we reached the head of the line, I knew I was making a mistake. But I had to get into the car.

I gulped hard as the coaster rolled forward. Climbing the first hill, I closed my eyes and prayed. But my prayer didn't resemble Jehoshaphat's when he was afraid. Instead, I prayed that the ride would end and that I'd survive it. God answered in an unexpected way. I not only survived; I was hooked on roller coasters! (They are still my favorite amusement park ride.)

Since that day almost 20 years ago, I've learned to pray differently when I'm afraid. I don't always remember to follow Jehoshaphat's pattern. But when I do, God relieves the fear and gives me courage to face the situation that caused it.

Like David, Jehoshaphat knew the value of praise. (See Study 3.) It's easier to confront our fears after we've focused our attention on God who "rule[s] over all the kingdoms of the nations" and who possesses power and might greater than anyone or anything that instills fear. "When I am afraid," David wrote in another psalm, "I will trust in you. In God, whose word I praise, in God I trust; I will not be afraid" (Psalm 56:3-4).

With his focus on God, Jehoshaphat recalled a previous time when God had rescued His people from a similar situation. This look at history further cemented his confidence in God's ability to deal with the present problem.

In addition, Jehoshaphat relied on God's promises. God had already said He would inhabit the Temple and that He would give the land to Abraham's descendant forever. So Jehoshaphat knew that no foreign army could permanently defeat them.

Today we have a Bible full of promises on which to rely. Isaiah, for example, tells us, "So do not fear, for I am with you; do not be dismayed, for I am your God. I will strengthen you and help you; I will uphold you with my righteous right hand" (41:10).

It wasn't until Jehoshaphat had filled his mind and heart with God's character, actions, and promises that he told God about his problem and asked for help. In response, God reassured him and the people through the prophet Jahaziel. God's message of hope to Jehoshaphat is one we can still claim today when we're afraid: "Do not be afraid or discouraged. . . . For the battle is not yours but God's" (v. 15).

Did you notice Jehoshaphat's unusual battle strategy—praise? That same method enables us today to win the victory over whatever causes us fear. So what do you fear? Instead of focusing on that situation or person, praise the Lord. God may not solve the problem immediately, but the praise will sustain you until He does.

USING THE PATTERN

Think about your greatest fear. Then record your prayer, following Jehoshaphat's pattern.

❦ Praise God for who He is and what He is like.

❦ Reflect on what God has done for you in the past.

❦ Express your confidence in God's ability to hear and answer your prayer.

❦ State your fear.

❦ Ask God to help you overcome the situation that is causing this fear. Acknowledge your own powerlessness and lack of wisdom.

To practice this prayer pattern during the week, use these guidelines. Summarize or write out your prayers below.

Day 1   Think about characteristics of God that you need to remember when you're afraid. Praise Him for what He is like.

Day 2   Think about specific ways God has helped you in the past. Thank Him.

Day 3   Tell God why you are confident that He will help you again. Remind Him of pertinent promises.

Day 4   Talk to God about your fears. God understands and wants to help you.

Day 5   Pray for God's power and wisdom to conquer your fears.

6

WHEN YOU'RE PERPLEXED

Habakkuk 3

❧

EXAMINING THE PATTERN

1. What are your first thoughts when you face a crisis?

Compare yourself to Habakkuk as you complete this study. God called Habakkuk to announce Nebuchadnezzar's invasion of Judah in 605 B.C. God planned to allow Nebuchadnezzar to deport the Judean population to Babylon as punishment for sin. This situation perplexed Habakkuk, so he asked God two questions.
Read Habakkuk 1–2.
  2. What was Habakkuk's first question? (1:2-4)

What was God's answer? (1:5-11)

3. What was Habakkuk's second question? (1:12–2:1)

What was God's answer?

In light of these perplexing problems, Habakkuk prayed.
Read Habakkuk 3:1-2.
  4. What did Habakkuk acknowledge as he began this prayer? Why?

5. What did he ask God to do? (Note: The deeds he referred to are described in 1:5-11.)

6. Why would Habakkuk make this request?

Read Habakkuk 3:3-15.
7. How did Habakkuk describe God?

8. What are some of the past events to which Habakkuk referred? Skim these passages: Exodus 7:14–15:21; 19:1–21:1; Joshua 10:12-14.

9. Why do you think Habakkuk reflected on these particular works of God?

Read Habakkuk 3:16-19.
10. Why did Habakkuk tremble at this description of God and His past works?

11. What would the impending invasion do to the land of Judah?

12. How did Habakkuk respond to this coming disaster?

13. Why could he express joy in these perplexing and troubling circumstances?

14. What did God do for Habakkuk?

15. What perplexing circumstances are you facing today?

16. How does your attitude toward those circumstances compare with Habakkuk's?

17. On what or on whom are you depending for your joy?

18. How can you exult in the Lord today in spite of your circumstances?

19. Now that you've studied Habakkuk's pattern, identify a change you need to make in the way you pray. Write it on page 72, *Changing the Pattern of My Prayers.*

FITTING THE PATTERN

Habakkuk had every right to feel perplexed. What a confusing situation! But unlike so many of us today, Habakkuk was willing to leave himself and the situation in God's hands. Instead of fretting, he trusted. And he prayed—giving us a pattern for our prayers when life comes crashing in.

First Habakkuk expressed his fear. "I stand in awe of your deeds, O Lord" (3:2). He was afraid of what God would do because he knew God's power. Then Habakkuk presented two requests. First, he wanted to see a fresh show of God's power, a renewal of His intervention in the face of the Babylonian invasion. Second, he asked for mercy in God's judgment. When Habakkuk glimpsed the future, he saw that without God's mercy, there was the potential for total destruction.

After making his requests, Habakkuk didn't rehearse a litany of what was wrong. Instead, he remembered God's great works of the past. And as he thought about God's power, he became an emotional wreck: "I heard and my heart pounded, my lips quivered at the sound; decay crept into my bones, and my legs trembled" (v. 16). Habakkuk demonstrated that we don't have to have our emotions under control at all times. It's OK to break down before God; God understands. He won't berate us for doing so.

But still Habakkuk trusted God. In the face of promised total economic disaster, Habakkuk declared exuberant joy and drew his strength from the Lord. Habakkuk's attitude did not depend on circumstances or on what God gives. No matter what would happen, Habakkuk *chose* to rejoice. His response echoes Paul's letter to the Philippians: "I have learned the secret of being content in any and every situation, whether well fed or hungry, whether living in plenty or in want. I can do everything through him who gives me strength" (Philippians 4:12b-13). And in verse 4 Paul writes, "Rejoice in the Lord always. I will say it again: Rejoice!" Will you?

USING THE PATTERN

As you face circumstances you don't understand, pattern your prayer after Habakkuk's.

❦ Express your emotions.

❦ Make your request.

❦ Describe God and His past dealings in your life that are related to your present problems.

❦ Determine to draw your joy and strength from God in spite of your circumstances.

Continue to pray like Habakkuk did as you deal with present crises or in preparation for perplexing situations to come. Summarize or write out your prayers below.

Day 1   Talk to God about how you're feeling. Don't try to cover up your emotions; He knows them anyway.

Day 2   What do you want God to do about the crises in your life? Tell Him.

Day 3   Describe God as you know Him. Make those descriptions your praise to Him.

Day 4   Rehearse what God has done for you in crisis situations; then thank Him.

Day 5   Choose to rejoice in the Lord and draw your strength from Him. Tell Him so.

7

WHEN YOU FEEL WORTHLESS

Psalm 139

❧

EXAMINING THE PATTERN

1. What makes you feel worthless? Why?

2. On what do people normally focus when they feel worthless?

Compare this focus with David's as you read Psalm 139. Read verses 1-6.
3. What point was David making as he began to pray?

4. What did God know about him?

5. How did David respond to this knowledge?

6. How would a rehearsal of God's knowledge about yourself affect your view of yourself?

Read verses 7-12.
7. To what did David shift his focus as he continued praying?

8. Why is this attribute, or characteristic, of God comforting for someone who feels worthless?

Read verses 13-18.

9. David then turned to God's power. In what specific way does God demonstrate power?

10. David said that God personally put together our chromosomes in our mothers' wombs. How does this affect your feelings about any physical or mental problems you experience?

   About a retarded or deformed child, sibling, or acquaintance?

   What could you do about the "handicaps" above that would reflect God's creative love?

11. "All the days ordained for me were written in your book before one of them came to be," David wrote in verse 16. Make some notes below regarding people, events, and feelings as they relate to your own days.

   ❧ yesterday's disappointments and struggles

   ❧ today's schedule and unplanned interruptions

   ❧ uncertainties about your future

❦ the loss of your job

❦ the loss of your mate through death or divorce

❦ the "premature" death of a child or friend

❦ a parent or elderly friend who suffers physically and wants to die

Since God ordained even these days before you were born, how can you begin to live out that knowledge in some of the situations above?

12. How does reflecting on God's power in human creation affect your sense of self-worth?

13. How did David respond? Why?

14. How would verses 17 and 18 affect someone who feels worthless?

Read verses 19-24.

15. David concluded his prayer by focusing on one more attribute of God. What is it?

16. Why would David shift to concern about wicked people and their evil behavior?

17. How does this concern fit his knowledge of God as all-knowing, all-present, and all-powerful?

18. Meditate on verses 23 and 24. How do they relate to the way we view ourselves?

19. How does focusing on God's character help when we feel worthless?

20. In what specific ways does this prayer encourage you?

21. Now that you've studied David's pattern, identify a change you need to make in the way you pray. Write it on page 72, *Changing the Pattern of My Prayers.*

FITTING THE PATTERN

If you were to measure your worth in coins, which would you choose: pennies, nickels, dimes, quarters, silver dollars, or Olympic commemorative gold coins? Which would God choose?

According to Psalm 139, God would definitely choose the gold coins. In His eyes, each of us is of infinite worth. So David's prayer provides an appropriate pattern for us when we feel worthless.

To gain a biblical perspective of our true worth, we need to focus on four characteristics of God. First, God is omniscient. He knows everything about us — our actions, our thoughts, our destinations, our words. And He still loves us and wants to be with us! (See John 3:16; Romans 5:18; and 1 John 3:1.) That knowledge should be enough to convince us that we have worth.

But David did not stop there. Second, he focused on God's omnipresence. There is no place on earth, in heaven, or in sheol (the place of wicked dead) where we can escape from God. God is always with us. People who spend a lot of time with us do so because they enjoy our company. We are of value to them.

Next David praised God because He is omnipotent, or all-powerful. He designed us even before we were conceived. That's power! It's also an indicator of worth. As Paul wrote in Ephesians 2:10, "We are God's workmanship, created in Christ Jesus to do good works, which God prepared in advance for us to do." After all, would the God of the universe take the time and effort to do such detailed creation if we were of no value?

Finally, David turned his attention to God's holiness. On the surface, it seems like David made a huge leap from God's design of him before birth to asking for judgment on the wicked. But this progression is logical if we consider the context.

> David has just considered the wonder of God's knowledge, presence, and power. If God has all these wonderful attributes, why is evil so successful in this world? God knows all things, and God can do all things! Yet, God seems to be doing nothing! ... As New Testament Christians, we realize that God has settled the sin problem at the cross, that He Himself has suffered for us, so that we cannot accuse Him of not doing anything. But the Old Testament believer did not have the benefit of this clear understanding. . . .
>
> The psalmist's views of sins and judgment were not false, but neither were they complete. Because we have the Epistle to the Romans, we can understand better how God can be patient with the rebel and (seemingly) not punish sin during this Gospel age of reconciliation (Warren W. Wiersbe, *Meet Yourself in the Psalms*, Victor Books, 1983, pp. 139–140).

As David aligned himself with God and drew his self worth from that relationship, he acknowledged that God's enemies were also his enemies. Therefore, he wanted to be separate from violent, evil men. Like God, he hated, or disapproved of, their conduct. And he did not want to be drawn into their lifestyle.

Since we are of value to God, we should want to please Him. Pleasing God involves viewing sin as God does and desiring to get rid of any sin in our lives. Thus David ended his prayer with a plea for God to search his heart: "Search me, O God, and know my heart; test me and know my anxious thoughts. See if there is any offensive way in me, and lead me in the way everlasting" (Psalm 139:23-24).

So the next time you feel worthless, read Psalm 139. It's a great antidote for an unbiblical view of yourself.

USING THE PATTERN

Think about a time when you felt worthless. Then write a prayer after David's pattern to focus your thoughts on God instead of on yourself.

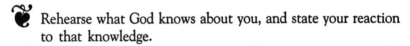 Rehearse what God knows about you, and state your reaction to that knowledge.

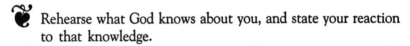 Rehearse where God is and how His presence affects you.

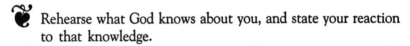 State examples of God's power and your reaction to them.

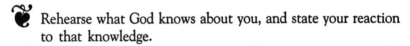 Reflect specifically on the fact that God designed you physically and mentally and ordained your days before you were conceived.

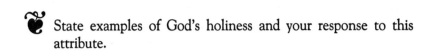 State examples of God's holiness and your response to this attribute.

Combat feelings of worthlessness by practicing David's prayer pattern. Summarize or write out your prayers below.

Day 1   Review what happened to you yesterday. In light of those events and your responses, talk to God about what He knows about you.

Day 2   Discuss with God how His omniscience, or all-knowing, makes you feel. Ask Him to turn any fears into comfort.

Day 3   Think through today's schedule. Thank God that He will be with you at all times and that He already planned this day. Discuss your feelings about unexpected interruptions and problems.

Day 4   Thank God for His power on your behalf, particularly for what He did before you were born.

Day 5   Pray Psalm 139:23-24, "Search me, O God, and know my heart; test me and know my anxious thoughts. See if there is any offensive way in me, and lead me in the way everlasting." Spend time listening for God's answer.

8

WHEN FRIENDS ARE WEAK

Ephesians 3:14-21

Examining the Pattern

1. When one of your Christian friends is spiritually weak, what do you pray for her or him?

2. How do you pray for yourself when you lack power to obey God?

Compare your prayers with Paul's as you read Ephesians 3:14-21.
3. What all did Paul ask God the Father to do for the Ephesians?

4. On what basis did he make these requests?

5. Why do you think Paul appealed to this basis?

6. How does God answer this kind of prayer today? Be specific.

7. What did Paul trust would result from this request? Put each result in your own words, then give an example of a specific evidence of it in daily life.

8. How would the granting of Paul's request build up these believers?

Reread verses 20-21.
9. How does this final sentence bring closure to Paul's requests?

10. What do you learn about God from these verses?

11. How would this ending to Paul's prayer build up weak believers?

12. What was most important to Paul when he prayed for the Ephesians?

13. What would you expect him to pray that he didn't?

14. Which of your friends lacks God's power? In what areas?

15. How is the focus of this prayer different from the way you normally pray for weak friends?

16. In what specific ways would this prayer build up your friends?

17. Now that you've studied Paul's pattern, identify a change you need to make in the way you pray. Write it on page 72, *Changing the Pattern of My Prayers.*

FITTING THE PATTERN

Power. The quest for it is prominent in our culture. Businessmen wear power ties and power suits. Company executives and salespeople do power lunches. Men and women vie for positions of power within organizations.

Christians hunger for power too. Almost every church has one or more persons who are the power brokers. They may or may not hold leadership positions, but they sway decisions and heavily influence others. Ministry directors plan powerful programs, and we expect a steady diet of powerful sermons from our pastors. We even buy books with powerful titles, such as *Power Evangelism, Power Healing,* and *Power Religion.*

In spite of this emphasis on power, we still struggle with spiritual weaknesses. We give in to temptation, often without a fight. We make excuses for our lack of commitment to God and our local churches. Perhaps we're pursuing the wrong kind of power. Perhaps we're ignorant of God's available power. Or perhaps sin blocks His power in us. Whatever the reason, Paul's prayer for God's enablement in believers is a powerful (pun intended) pattern for us today.

Paul prayed twice for the Ephesian believers to experience God's power. Power was available to them, but apparently they weren't using it. Paul pointed out that this power is imparted through the person of the Holy Spirit as Christ had promised: "But you will receive power when the Holy Spirit comes on you" (Acts 1:8). God may choose, however, not to release that power in the presence of unconfessed sin. (See Ephesians 4:29–5:2.)

Furthermore, this power is released in proportion to God's riches — making it unlimited. Certainly, there is enough power for the greatest weakness with which we struggle.

Along with this request, Paul prayed for three aspects of spiritual growth to accompany this power. First, when God empowers His children, Christ feels at home in them, "so that Christ may dwell in your hearts through faith" (v. 17). This word picture indicates "not a surface relationship, but an ever-deepening fellowship" (Warren W. Wiersbe, *Be Rich,* Wheaton, IL: Victor Books, 1976, p. 85).

Second, he wanted these believers "to grasp how wide and long and high and deep is the love of Christ, and to know this love that surpasses knowledge"(vv. 18-19). To grasp Christ's abundant love is to experience it firsthand. Paul wanted them to develop a greater appreciation of all God offers through faith in Christ.

Finally, Paul asked for God's fullness, desiring that the Ephesians be dominated by God.

God's fullness is that with which He is filled, and denotes the perfections and excellencies He possesses. . . . He is the unlimited source from which we draw for all the spiritual resources we need (Homer A. Kent, Jr., *Ephesians: The Glory of the Church,* Chicago: Moody Press, 1971, pp. 60-61).

In light of the greatness of God's power, Paul broke out in praise to God. God can do more for us than we can ever imagine. Therefore, He rightly deserves such praise. So when you and your friends lack the strength to gain victory over Satan's temptations and to serve God, use Paul's prayer pattern. All the power we need is available if we ask for it.

USING THE PATTERN

As you pray for friends who are weak, record your requests in the following pattern.

🐦 Make your request, along with the basis on which you're asking.

🐦 Identify the spiritual growth you would like to see happen as a result of this request.

🐦 Praise God, identifying specific abilities that enable Him to grant your request.

Continue to practice this prayer pattern for friends who need God's power, as well as for yourself. Summarize or write out your prayers on page 57.

Day 1   Meditate on God's power and specific ways He shows it. Praise Him for being all-powerful; thank Him for willingly sharing His power with us.

Day 2   Ask God to make you aware of friends who lack power to live for Him.

Day 3   Pray that God will strengthen your friends with His power. Identify areas of spiritual growth that you'd like to see as a result.

Day 4   Pray for yourself—as you prayed for friends yesterday.

Day 5   Praise God with the words of Ephesians 3:20-21: "Now to him who is able to do immeasurably more than all we ask or imagine, according to his power that is at work within us, to him be glory in the church and in Christ Jesus throughout all generations, for ever and ever! Amen."

9

WHEN YOU WANT BELIEVERS TO GROW

Ephesians 1:15-23; Philippians 1:9-11; Colossians 1:9-12

☙

EXAMINING THE PATTERN

1. When you pray for your Christian friends, for what do you pray the most? (Check one.)

____ health, physical needs
____ money
____ work
____ relationships
____ spiritual growth
____ specific problems
____ other _____

Notice what your prayers have in common with Paul's when he prayed for fellow believers.
Read Ephesians 1:15-23.
2. Why did Paul pray for these believers? Skim verses 3-14.

3. Why did Paul thank God for them?

4. What was Paul's first request for the Ephesian believers? Explain it in your own words.

5. What was his second request? What did he mean?

6. What three results would come as the answer to this request?

7. What example of these results did Paul give?

8. Why was this example appropriate for his request?

9. How would these two requests help the Ephesians grow spiritually?

Read Philippians 1:9-11.
10. What did Paul request for these believers?

11. How would they grow when God answered this request?

12. How do we "discern what is best"?

13. Why do you think Paul prayed like this?

Read Colossians 1:9-12.
14. What did Paul ask God to do for the Colossian believers?

15. What specific results did he want to see from this request? Give an example of each.

16. How would this request help the Colossian believers grow spiritually?

17. How do these prayers compare with yours for the spiritual growth of your friends? Which requests are similar? Which ones are different?

18. What do you think would happen to your friends if you prayed like this for them?

    What do you think would happen if you prayed like this for yourself?

19. Now that you've studied Paul's pattern, identify a change you need to make in the way you pray. Write it on page 72, *Changing the Pattern of My Prayers.*

FITTING THE PATTERN

Think about the last time you participated in group prayer. For what were most of the requests? The bulk of my church prayer meeting experiences differ greatly from Paul's prayers. Most of the requests center on physical needs — health, money, things, places to live. Asking for spiritual growth seems to be taboo. Perhaps this situation exists because it's scary to expose our inner needs to the scrutiny of others. But until we learn to pray for one another at that level, we will continue to cheat ourselves of significant growth. Paul's prayers for the believers to whom he wrote provide several requests that we can personalize for our friends, study groups, and congregations as well as for ourselves. His requests included the following:

❦ *Better knowledge of God.* The word *knowledge* refers to an experiential knowledge. It is more than knowing facts about God; it is growing a relationship with Him. This kind of knowledge develops as we read and study the Bible, as we observe God's creation (see also Romans 1:20), as we spend time with God in prayer, as we live in fellowship with Him.

Consequently, we can pray that our friends (and ourselves) will make Bible study and prayer a daily priority, that they will intentionally make time to spend with Him, and that the time will help them get to know God more intimately. We can pray that God will reveal His majesty and creativity when our friends take vacations and plan seemingly ordinary outdoor activities, such as picnics in the woods and afternoons at the beach. We can pray that they will practice God's presence all day long in the routine as well as the surprises. (See *Practicing the Presence of God* by Brother Andrew.

🐞 *Minds and hearts that are enlightened, or know the truth.* As a result, we will be aware of the hope of our calling, of Christ's return for us, of God's investment in us as His inheritance, and of God's power, energy, and strength. All of this is available for the asking.

So we can ask God to give our friends assurance of their salvation if they struggle with this issue. We can pray that they will look forward to their future with God, that this hope will keep them persevering in the midst of problems and pressures. We can pray that God will give them power to experience victory over temptation to sin, that He will energize them when they feel weak and tired, that He will strengthen them to accomplish the tasks before them.

🐞 *Love that abounds in knowledge and insight.* This will enable us to choose the best over what is good, to be pure and blameless, and to develop Christian character.

As we pray for our fellow believers, we need to ask God to increase their love for others, that He will help them grow the fruit of the Spirit (Galatians 5:22-23), that Paul's description of love in 1 Corinthians 13 will become a reality in their lives. (In fact, you may want to insert a friend's name for the word *love* and its pronoun *it* in that chapter, especially 1 Corinthians 13:4-8a, and pray through those verses.) For example, "Help Chris to be patient and kind, not to envy, not to boast, not to be proud."

Pray that your friends will have biblical discernment as they make choices and decisions, that their motives and attitudes will be pure instead of selfish or sinful and not cause others to stumble in their walks with the Lord. Also pray that they will increasingly become more like Christ.

❧ *Knowledge of God's will.* This knowledge will help us to live fruitful lives worthy of the Lord, to please Him in every way, to keep increasing in our knowledge of God, to be strengthened with His power, and to give thanks to God. Again, the word *knowledge* refers to experiential knowledge, knowing and prac-ticing God's Word. God has revealed His will in His Word, and we need to pray that we and fellow believers will spend time studying the Bible to discover His will and then obey it. Pray that obedience will lead to serving God and others, which will lead to spiritual growth, which will then lead to thankfulness, which is God's will (1 Thessalonians 5:18).

By praying for spiritual growth as Paul did, we can expect God to turn lives inside out and conform them to Himself. What a revival that will be!

USING THE PATTERN

As you pray for the growth of your Christian friends, follow Paul's pattern by recording your prayer below.

❧ State the reason/basis for your requests.

❧ Make your requests, focusing on biblical growth.

❧ State the results you would like to see in your friends' lives.

Practice this pattern through the week with these suggestions. Summarize or write out your prayers below.

Day 1   Praise God for what He has done for us. Be specific.

Day 2   Choose two or three friends. Pray for specific spiritual growth and results you would like to see in their lives.

Day 3   Repeat day 2 for several other friends.

Day 4   Repeat day 2 for yourself.

Day 5   Pray Philippians 1:9-11 for the people in your study group and/or your congregation, "And this is my prayer: that your love may abound more and more in knowledge and depth of insight, so that you may be able to discern what is best and may be pure and blameless until the day of Christ, filled with the fruit of righteousness that comes through Jesus Christ—to the glory and praise of God."

10

WHEN YOU'RE CONCERNED ABOUT THE FUTURE

Psalm 90

EXAMINING THE PATTERN

1. What concerns do you have about the future?

2. How have you been praying about these concerns?

As you read Moses' prayer in Psalm 90, compare it with yours in this area.
3. What mental pictures do the first few verses give you?

4. What do you learn about God from these verses?

5. How can this knowledge help you cope with concerns about the future?

6. After praising God, what did Moses focus on?

7. Why is this a natural progression?

8. In light of man's sin, why is verse 12 an appropriate request?

9. How can verse 12 help you cope with concerns about the future?

10. In light of what Moses prayed in verses 1-12, what would you expect him to say next?

11. What requests did he make? Why?

12. How are these requests related to concerns about the future?

13. Meditate on verses 1-2. How do they put concerns about the future into proper perspective?

14. About what areas of the future would you like to be less concerned?

15. How can using Moses' prayer pattern help you to do so?

16. Now that you've studied Moses' pattern, identify a change you need to make in the way you pray. Write it on page 72, *Changing the Pattern of My Prayers.*

FITTING THE PATTERN

Will I succeed at my job? Will my home business fail?

How can we afford to buy a house for our growing family? Or a new car to replace the one that needs too many repairs?

What will I do when my mother can no longer live by herself?

What will happen if Jim loses his job like so many others in his company?

What will I do if I find drugs in my son's dresser drawer?

What if I never meet Mr. Right and get married?

What if Carl divorces me like Larry did Diane?

What if my child gets sick? Or dies?

What if my children abandon the faith I have taught them?

Uncertainty about the future haunts us everywhere. Even as believers, we worry about what might—or might not—happen, replaying "what-if" scenarios in our minds and prayers.

Moses knew about this kind of uncertainty. He led the Israelites out of Egypt and through the Red Sea into the unknown. Then he wandered in the wilderness with them while they grumbled, complained, and rebelled. All Moses knew was that they were heading for the land God promised them. He didn't know how long it would take to get there or even exactly where it was. Moses had plenty of time and causes to play what-if scenarios.

Moses probably wrote the prayer recorded in Psalm 90 near the end of his life. After forty miserable years in the wilderness, he could not even enter the Promised Land because of a sin he had committed earlier. So now Moses faced the uncertainty of what he would do when the people entered without him. He may not have known that he was soon to die.

But Moses knew God. And his prayer offers us a pattern to follow when the future is uncertain and when our minds dwell on what-ifs.

Instead of beginning by complaining about the uncertainty of the future (as we often do), Moses thought first about God and praised Him:

> Lord, you have been our dwelling place
> throughout all generations.
> Before the mountains were born
> or you brought forth the earth and the world,
> from everlasting to everlasting you are God.
> —Psalm 90:1-2

Because God is unchanging, eternal, and sovereign, we don't need to let what-ifs rob us of our peace. God is in control of the future as well as the present. And wherever God is, we can be at home and experience security.

In contrast to God, Moses recognized that his life–like all of mankind's–was short. No one knows when he or she will die. Consequently, it is important to confess sins. We do this to prepare to meet God and even to avoid a premature death. (See 1 John 5:16.)

Brevity of life should also cause us to live wisely in light of eternity. Thus Moses began his requests with "Teach us to number our days aright, that we may gain a heart of wisdom" (v. 12). If we direct our energies and attentions to concerns that may never develop in the future, we lose the opportunities God gives us today. Jesus said, "Therefore do not worry about tomorrow, for tomorrow will worry about itself. Each day has enough trouble of its own" (Matthew 6:34).

Albert Barnes, writing in *Notes on the Old Testament*, comments,

> "If any one knew when, and where, and how he was to die, it might be presumed that this would exert an important influence on him in forming his plans, and on his general manner of life. The prayer is, that God would enable us to act as if we had such a view. (Albert Barnes, ed. by Robert Frew, *Notes on the Old Testament: Psalms*, Vol. III, Grand Rapids, MI: Baker Book House, 1950, p. 9).

Then Moses asked for God's compassion, love, joy, and favor—qualities tied to the present, not to the what-ifs of the future. He ended by requesting God's help to carry out his plans, an expression of dependence on God and an antidote for anxiety about what might happen.

Throughout this prayer, Moses ignores possible what-ifs about the future and concentrates instead on how to live now. So when you're concerned about the future, focus instead on the present. As a result, you'll be better prepared for whatever God has planned next.

USING THE PATTERN

As you pray about your concerns for the future, follow Moses' pattern. Record your prayer below.

❧ Praise God for His characteristics and works as they relate to the future.

❦ Confess any sin in your life.

❦ Make your requests, focusing on present growth that will prepare you for your future with God.

Use the following guidelines to practice Moses' prayer pattern. Summarize or write out your prayers below.

Day 1   Praise God that He is eternal and sovereign, knowing and controlling the future.

Day 2   Ask God to help you remember that He is your dwelling place, that since He is with you, you needn't feel unduly concerned about the future.

Day 3   Ask God to point out any unconfessed sin in your life; then deal with it.

Day 4   Pray Psalm 90:12: "Teach us to number our days aright, that we may gain a heart of wisdom." Ask God for wisdom to make the most of life now, no matter what the future holds.

Day 5   Tell God your requests as they relate to the future.

CHANGING THE PATTERN
OF MY PRAYERS

List changes you need to make in your prayers.

Study 1

Study 2

Study 3

Study 4

Study 5

Study 6

Study 7

Study 8

Study 9

Study 10

INTRODUCTION

Leading *Prayer Patterns*
Before the first group meeting, read through the *Contents* page and *Introduction* to get an overview of this study.

Each week try to read at least one commentary on the Scripture passage. Although this study focuses on the structure of the prayers and application for our prayer times, group members may ask other questions about the meaning of specific phrases. Don't be afraid to say "I don't know" to such questions. But do make an effort to report answers the next time you meet.

The *Group Study Guide* for each study incorporates a few questions from the study section. If you have time, share responses to more questions. Your members will benefit from the insights of others in the group.

Each session ends with group prayer based on the pattern studied as outlined in the *Fitting the Pattern* section. This repetition will help participants make the biblical patterns part of their private prayer times. For variety, you may want to have group members pray in pairs or triads at times instead of praying together as an entire group.

In sessions 2, 3, 5, and 8, songs and a booklet are suggested. Begin now to obtain these. You may be able to borrow cassettes from friends so you don't have to buy them.

This book may be used in a group Bible study in two ways.

Completing the Study Together
If most group members do not complete the Bible study before each session, work through the questions in *Examining the Pattern* together.

Incorporate other questions and suggestions from the *Group Study Guide* section at the appropriate times. If the study questions are personal, you may want to have everyone write down their answers instead of responding aloud. As the participants get to know one another better, however, they will find it safe to share personal information so others can pray for them.

Assign the *Fitting the Pattern* and *Using the Pattern* sections to be read and completed after the session. Use the *Group Prayer* suggestion from this *Group Study Guide* to close each session.

Group Study Guide Plan

The following plan assumes that most group members have completed the questions in the *Examining the Pattern* section, read the narrative commentary in *Fitting the Pattern*, and practiced using some of the prayer pattern with the suggestions in *Using the Pattern* prior to meeting together for group discussion.

More Tips for Leaders

Preparation
- ❦ Pray for the Holy Spirit's guidance as you prepare, so you will be equipped to lead the lesson and make it applicable. Pray for your participants personally; ask God to help them as they work through the study prior to the session; and pray for the impact of the meeting itself.
- ❦ Gather and/or prepare any materials you or the group will need for the meeting.
- ❦ Read through the entire lesson and related Scriptures. Answer the questions for yourself.

The Meeting
- ❦ Start and end on time.
- ❦ Have group members wear name tags during meetings until they know one another's names.
- ❦ Spend the first 5–15 minutes of the initial meeting introducing yourselves, if this is necessary. Otherwise, spend some time answering a question that will help your group build a sense of community. (See samples on page 75.) In fact, you may use any good activity to help members get acquainted, interact with each other, or feel that they belong.

Community Builder Questions
Community builders help your people become better acquainted over the course of the study. If the group members don't know each other well, choose questions that are general or nonthreatening. As time goes by, questions may become more specific or focused. Reassure the members that they may pass on any question they feel is too personal. Choose from these samples or create your own.

> *What do you like to do for fun?*
> *What is your favorite season? Dessert? Book?*
> *What would be your ideal vacation?*
> *What exciting thing happened to you this week?*
> *What was the most memorable activity you did with your family when you were a child?*
> *Name three things you are thankful for.*
> *Imagine that your home is on fire. What three items would you try to take with you as you escaped?*
> *If you were granted one wish, what would it be?*
> *Name the quality you appreciate most in a friend.*
> *What is your pet peeve?*
> *What is your greatest hope? Greatest fear?*
> *What is your greatest accomplishment? Greatest disappointment?*

The Discussion
In discussion, members should interact not only with you, the group leader, but with one another. Usually you will start the ball rolling by asking a question to which there is more than a single acceptable answer. You are also responsible for keeping the discussion on track because if it gets out of hand and rambles, it loses much of its value.

Here are some guidelines for leading discussion:
- Maintain a relaxed, informal atmosphere.
- Encourage everyone to take part, but don't call on people by name unless you are sure they are willing to participate.
- Give members enough time to reflect and answer a question. If necessary, restate it.
- If someone is shy, ask that person to answer an opinion question or another nonthreatening question.
- Acknowledge any contribution, regardless of merit.
- Don't correct or embarrass a person who gives a wrong answer. Thank the person; then ask, "What do the rest of you think?"

❧ If someone monopolizes the discussion, say, "On the next question, let's hear from someone who hasn't spoken yet." Or sit next to the monopolizer to avoid encouraging her with eye contact.

❧ If someone goes off on a tangent, wait for the person to draw a breath, then say, "Thanks for those interesting comments. Now let's get back to . . . " and mention the subject or passage under consideration. Sometimes merely restating a question will bring the discussion back on target.

❧ If someone asks a question, allow others in the group to give their answers before you offer yours.

❧ Summarize the discussion after the contributions cease and before you move on.

❧ Include in your meeting a time for sharing lessons which group members learn in their personal study time, praise items, prayer requests and answers, as well as a time for prayer itself.

WHEN YOU WANT TO IMPROVE YOUR PRAYER LIFE

Matthew 6:5-13

OBJECTIVE: To balance our prayer lives by incorporating the elements included in Christ's model prayer.

GROUP PARTICIPATION
1. What is one of your biggest struggles with prayer?
2. What kinds of balance do people normally try to make in their lives? Why is it difficult to maintain balance in our lives? Why is it important to try to do so?

Read aloud Matthew 6:5-13.
3. What are some of your favorite memories of this prayer?
4. Look at the two graphs on page 9. Where did you place yourself on them? Explain.
5. How do you feel about your "score" on the prayer graphs?
6. How are your usual prayers similar and how are they different from Christ's model prayer?
7. What elements of prayer did Jesus include in His model? Why do you think He included each one? Why do you think He put them in this order?
8. What kinds of prayer are missing from this model? Why do you think Jesus left these out?
9. Jesus worshiped God by saying, " 'Our Father in heaven, hallowed be your name.' " How do we hallow, or make holy, God's name?
10. Read verse 10 again. Why is submission to God's will important?
11. How is submission related to making requests of God?
12. Why do you think Jesus only requested food and not a long grocery list of requests like we tend to do?
13. What do you see in Christ's model prayer that you would like to influence your own praying?
14. Read and explain your response to one of the prayer patterns beginning on page 12.
15. If you were to set one prayer goal for the coming week, what would that goal be?

GROUP PRAYER

Use Christ's model as the structure for your prayer time. One at a time, read the six statements listed in *Using the Pattern*. After each, pause for a few minutes to pray short prayers relevant to that element. (Switch to silent prayer for the confession time.) Encourage everyone to participate in each section.

WHEN YOU'VE SINNED

Psalm 51

OBJECTIVE: To confess sin in the manner that David did.

GROUP PARTICIPATION

1. What kinds of sin are OK according to our society? Why?
2. What are some recent examples of public sins or private sins made public? How did people in general react to knowing about these sins?

Read aloud Psalm 51.

3. What was David's attitude toward sin?
4. How does David's attitude compare with yours?
5. David had sinned against Uriah, Bathsheba, and the soldiers in his army. Why, then, did he say in verse 4 of his prayer that he had sinned against God?
6. What is God like? Go around your circle at least once, with each person naming a different characteristic of God.
7. How does knowing that God is like what you just now described make it easier to confess your sin?
8. What different parts did you find in David's prayer of confession?
9. Which of these aspects of David's prayer of confession seem particularly important to you? Why?
10. After David confessed his sin, what did he ask God to do? Put his request in your own words.
11. What would David be able to do as a result of confessing his sin? Why did he have to confess first?
12. What have you seen people do to try to make up for some wrong that they have done?
13. What good comes from these atoning actions? In what ways are these actions also inadequate?
14. Why is confession to God the only way to receive real forgiveness for sin?
15. Listen to Margaret Becker's song "Just Come In" (*Immigrant's Daughter*, Sparrow). How does she express the futility of trying to atone for ourselves — and God's attitude after we confess?
16. How can David's prayer pattern help you when you sin?

GROUP PRAYER

Since confession of sin is a sensitive area for group prayer, use this pattern for silent response. One at a time, read the statements listed in *Using the Pattern*. After each, pause for a few minutes to pray silently. Then ask several volunteers to pray aloud that you will all be sensitive to sin and quick to use this pattern when needed.

WHEN YOU'RE GOING THROUGH TROUBLE

Psalm 138

OBJECTIVE: To praise the Lord even when we are going through trouble.

SPECIAL PREPARATION
Contact a group member who is expressive/dramatic to prepare the monologue described in #1 below.

GROUP PARTICIPATION
1. Have the prepared participant deliver a monologue to demonstrate how people usually pray when they are going through trials. Suggest that she include lots of descriptions of the problem, cries of help, and frantic statements of not knowing what to do.
2. Ask how many group members can identify with this prayer. Discuss why or why not.

Alternate Beginning: If someone were to secretly tape record your prayers during a time of trouble, what would that person hear? How do you feel about praying during times of trouble?

Read aloud Psalm 138.
3. Identify and explain the parts of David's prayer.
4. How did David praise God? For what reasons?
5. Describe God's love and faithfulness. How do these character qualities help us praise God?
6. Why will earthly rulers praise the Lord?
7. How can our praise reflect God's glory?
8. When David went through trials, of what was he confident? Why?
9. How can we experience the same confidence?
10. On what did David focus when he was going through a time of trouble?

11. How can David's focus help you when you face your own troubles?
12. Describe a time when God helped you during hardship or trouble. What did that experience teach you about God's character?
13. Pause to praise God together for the characteristics you have just mentioned. Take turns praying, "God, you are. . . ."
14. Why is praising the Lord an important element in prayer when we are going through trouble?
15. What changes have occurred when you have been able to praise God in spite of difficult circumstances? Changes in circumstances? Changes in yourself?
16. In what practical ways can you use David's prayer pattern this week?

GROUP PRAYER

Think of a current trial or problem with which you struggle. Then use David's pattern as the structure for your group prayer. One at a time, read the four statements listed in *Using the Pattern*. After each reading, pause for a few minutes to allow group members to pray short prayers relevant to that element. Encourage everyone to participate in each element.

Optional closing: Play the song "Praise the Lord" *(The Very Best of the Imperials,* Word). These lyrics help us see the power of praising God in times of trouble.

WHEN THINGS ARE GOING WELL

1 Chronicles 29:1-19

OBJECTIVE: To focus on praising God even when everything is going well.

GROUP PARTICIPATION
1. When everything is going well in your life, how do you pray? Use 3 or 4 chenille wires to construct a shape that illustrates how you pray at those times. Explain your design.
2. Why is it easy to become complacent in praying when everything is going well?

Read aloud 1 Chronicles 29:1-19.
3. What situation prompted David's prayer?
4. How did David combat a tendency toward complacency in his prayer?
5. Identify and explain each part of David's prayer.
6. What progression of topics do you notice in this prayer? Why do you think David put them in this order?
7. Look more carefully at verses 10-13. Why was this an appropriate way to begin?
8. For what did David specifically praise God?
9. How did the praise section of David's prayer relate to his circumstances?
10. Why is it helpful to focus our praise to correspond to the situation?
11. How did David describe himself and his relationship with God?
12. How do these descriptions fit the situation that prompted this prayer?
13. What did the requests David made to God suggest about the motives behind his gifts and his prayer?
14. When things are going well, what can we do to develop dependence on God instead of independence from God?
15. What impresses you most about this prayer? Why?
16. What do you need to add to the structure of your prayers to follow David's pattern?

GROUP PRAYER

Think about the good things God has been doing for you lately. Then use David's pattern as the structure for your prayer time. One at a time, read the statements listed in *Using the Pattern*. After each section, pause for a few minutes to allow group members to pray short prayers relevant to that element.

Group Study Guide 5

WHEN YOU'RE AFRAID

2 Chronicles 20:1-22

OBJECTIVE: To practice praising God in situations that cause fear.

GROUP PARTICIPATION
  1. Describe a situation in which you were afraid. What did you do at first? What did you do after the first moments of fear had past?
  2. If possible, play Don Francisco's song "Jehoshaphat" (*Forgiven*, NewPax).

Read aloud 2 Chronicles 20:1-12.
  3. Why do you think that praise has been so prominent in the prayer patterns we've studied so far?
  4. Study verses 6-12 of Jehoshaphat's prayer. Describe each section of the prayer.
  5. What do each of his descriptions tell us about God?
  6. How might each of these descriptions of God help you when you are afraid?
  7. How did Jehoshaphat's prayer reflect God's history with His people?
  8. On what basis did Jehoshaphat go to God? Why?
  9. Why was Jehoshaphat afraid?
  10. What did he ask God to do? Why?
  11. Describe his attitude toward God.
  12. Why do you think Jehoshaphat included praise in his battle plan?

Read aloud 2 Chronicles 20:13-22.
  13. When did God begin to work in this situation? Why do you think He responded at that point?
  14. Have you ever been able to praise God during a time of fear? If so, tell your group about the experience.
  15. What effect did praising God have on you? What response, if any, did you see from God?
  16. What have you learned from Jehoshaphat's prayer and God's answer that could help you when you're afraid?

GROUP PRAYER
Think about what makes you afraid. Then use Jehoshaphat's pattern

as the structure for your prayer time together. One at a time, read the statements listed in *Using the Pattern*. After each, pause for a few minutes to allow group members to pray short prayers relevant to that element.

WHEN YOU'RE PERPLEXED

Habakkuk 3

OBJECTIVE: To choose to rejoice in God no matter what happens.

SPECIAL PREPARATION

Before this session, write the statements from *Using the Pattern* on a half sheet of poster board or on the chalkboard. If on the latter, tape paper over the writing until it is time to read it.

GROUP PARTICIPATION

1. We live in a fast-paced era. What are some examples of "instants" in our society?
2. What influence is the instant society in which we live likely to have on our prayer patterns?

Habakkuk prayed the prayer we are about to study two years before the events happened. Read aloud Habakkuk 3.

3. What emotions does this prayer raise in you?
4. What hints of the passing of time do you find in Habakkuk's prayer?
5. Habakkuk did not pray in a vacuum. He remembered God's works in history. Why does remembering God's past with us build confidence for the future?
6. What have you learned from your own past experiences with God?
7. Spend a few minutes now reminding one another of who God is and what He has done on behalf of His people in your own setting.
8. What sections do you find in Habakkuk's prayer?
9. What does this prayer reveal about God? About man's relationship with Him?
10. Why do you think Habakkuk could express joy in such perplexing circumstances?
11. Would you have prayed like Habakkuk in this situation? Explain.
12. Rewrite Habakkuk 3:17. Use contemporary terms to express your own present circumstances. Then read your paraphrases aloud to each other.
13. What is one of the worst things that could happen to you?

14. Habakkuk prayed, "Though . . . yet I will rejoice in the Lord, I will be joyful in God my Savior. The Sovereign Lord is my strength" (vv. 18-19). Habakkuk's joy was not in the circumstances, but in God himself. If you are able to do so honestly, fill in the blank above with some of your own "worst things" circumstances. (What is happening or could happen to you?) Then, one at a time, pray the prayer aloud.

GROUP PRAYER
Practice Habakkuk's pattern during your prayer time. One at a time, read the statements listed on the poster or chalkboard. After each heading, pause for a few minutes to pray short prayers relevant to that element.

WHEN YOU FEEL WORTHLESS

Psalm 139

OBJECTIVE: To focus on God's character when we feel worthless.

SPECIAL PREPARATION
Bring aluminum foil for each person.

GROUP PARTICIPATION
1. Use about two feet of aluminum foil. Tear or sculpt an object representing something that makes you feel worthless. Explain your object.
2. What specific actions do people take in order to be liked by others? How well do these actions accomplish their goal?

David began his prayer with a word picture of God. Read aloud Psalm 139:1-6.

3. What was David's point here?
4. How does God's knowledge of you make you feel?
5. If God were writing a word picture of you, what do you think He would write?
6. How might a review of God's knowledge about yourself affect your view of yourself?

Read aloud Psalm 139:7-24.

7. Divide David's prayer into sections and give a title to each part.
8. Look more carefully at verses 7-12. Why could God's character, as it is described here, be comforting to someone who feels worthless?
9. Silently reread verses 13-18 inserting your own name in the appropriate places. If you were going through a period when your life seemed to lack purpose or value, how might this section of David's prayer influence your feelings? Your actions?
10. Since God designed us physically before we were born, can we blame Him for physical and mental deformities? Why or why not?
11. When have you experienced spiritual growth because of someone's physical or mental imperfections?
12. How could Psalm 139 help create a sense of self-worth in a person who was not physically or mentally "normal"?

13. People who read Psalm 139 sometimes omit verses 19-22. Why? Why do you think David included them in this prayer?
14. Why might the prayer of verses 23-24 be difficult to pray with honesty?
15. How does focusing on God's character help when we feel worthless?
16. In what specific ways does this prayer encourage you?

GROUP PRAYER

Pray together, using David's pattern. One at a time, read the statements listed in *Using the Pattern*. After each, pause for a few minutes to pray short prayers relevant to that element. Close by reading verses 23 and 24 together.

WHEN FRIENDS ARE WEAK

Ephesians 3:14-21

OBJECTIVE: To pray for God's empowerment that results in specific areas of growth for friends who are spiritually weak.

SPECIAL PREPARATION
Try to obtain a copy of the booklet *My Heart—Christ's Home* by Robert Boyd Munger (InterVarsity Press), and read it. If you don't have enough time during the group session to read it all, prepare to summarize it.

GROUP PARTICIPATION
1. When someone is spiritually weak, what signs do you see?
2. What are some causes of spiritual weakness?
3. How would you normally pray for someone who is spiritually weak? (Or would you?)

Read aloud Paul's prayer for weak believers in Ephesians 3:14-21.

4. What all did Paul ask the Father to do for the Ephesians?
5. On what basis did he make those requests?
6. Why do you think Paul appealed to that basis?
7. When have you seen God grant the kinds of requests Paul asked in this prayer?
8. Read or summarize *My Heart—Christ's Home* to illustrate Paul's request.
9. If you were to divide Paul's prayer for the Ephesians into sections, where would you put division points and what would you title each section?
10. How does the sentence in verses 20-21 bring closure to this prayer?
11. What do you learn about God from these verses? Why is it important to remember these characteristics when praying for friends who are spiritually weak? (or for yourself when you need strengthening?)
12. How is the focus of this prayer different from the way you normally pray?
13. How could this prayer strengthen people you know who are spiritually weak?

14. For whom do you need to pray this prayer?

GROUP PRAYER

Pray together, using Paul's pattern. One at a time, read the statements listed in *Using the Pattern*. After each, pause to pray short prayers relevant to that element. Encourage everyone to participate and to pray for themselves or for friends who are in need of God's power.

WHEN YOU WANT BELIEVERS TO GROW

Ephesians 1:15-23; Philippians 1:9-11; Colossians 1:9-12

OBJECTIVE: To state specific results when asking God for spiritual growth in others.

GROUP PARTICIPATION
1. Brainstorm the top ten requests we pray for fellow believers. List them on the chalkboard or a sheet of poster board. Then rate them in order of frequency.

Read some of Paul's prayers for growth in believers: Ephesians 1:15-23; Philippians 1:9-11; and Colossians 1:9-12.
2. What requests were on the top of Paul's list?
3. What was Paul's first request for the Ephesians believers? Explain it in your own words.
4. What was Paul's second request for the Ephesians? What do you think he meant?
5. What did Paul ask for the Philippian believers?
6. What did he ask for the Colossians? Why?
7. Identify and explain several sections in Paul's prayers.
8. When have you prayed for fellow believers like Paul did? (Or have you?) What results did you see?
9. Describe in your own words what a believer would be like after God granted Paul's requests.
10. Look again at Ephesians 1:15-23. What results did Paul hope to see in the Ephesians?
11. What did Paul hope to see in the Colossians? (See Colossians 1:9-12.)
12. How would the Philippians grow when God answered Paul's requests?
13. Why do you think Paul linked results to his requests?
14. What do you think could happen to your own friends if you regularly prayed for them in this way?

15. What changes would you expect if you regularly prayed these prayers for yourself?

GROUP PRAYER

Pray for yourselves, your study group, your congregation, and friends, using Paul's pattern. One at a time, read the statements listed in *Using the Pattern*. After each, pause for a few minutes to allow group members to pray short prayers relevant to that element.

Close your prayer time by selecting one of the three prayers. Then pray it for a friend, inserting his or her name. Or insert your own name.

WHEN YOU'RE CONCERNED ABOUT THE FUTURE

Psalm 90

OBJECTIVE: To praise God and ask for present growth to prepare for the future.

1. What concerns do you have about the future?
2. Why do we so often think in "what-if" terms about the future? **Read aloud Psalm 90 to review how Moses' prayer pattern can counteract our worries about the future.**
3. Identify and explain the parts Moses included in this prayer.
4. What mental picture do the first few verses give you?
5. What do you learn about God from verses 1-6?
6. How can this knowledge about God help you cope with your own concerns about the future?
7. Why do you think Moses began his prayer this way?
8. Find as many references as you can throughout the prayer to the passing of time.
9. What do you find in these descriptions of time that might ease your worries about the future?
10. What requests did Moses ask of God? Why?
11. How are these requests related to concerns about the future?
12. In a prayer that speaks so eloquently about the passing of time, why do you think Moses ends with something as mundane as work? (v. 17)
13. What work of your own do you hope that God will "establish?"
14. How can using Moses' prayer pattern help you be less concerned about the future?

GROUP PRAYER
Think back to the concern about the future that you identified at the beginning of this session. Then use Moses' pattern as the structure for your prayer time. One at a time, read the three statements listed in *Using the Pattern.* After each, pause for a few minutes to pray short

prayers relevant to that element. Have a time of silent prayer during the confession statement.

REVIEW TOGETHER
Take a few minutes for testimonies as you end this study. What have you learned from these ten sessions on the study of prayer?

How has it influenced your prayer times? In what specific ways has God used this study for your good?

What do you want to continue practicing as you spend time with God in prayer?